CLEVELAND

GUARDIANS

BY ANTHONY K. HEWSON

SportsZone

An Imprint of Abdo Publishing
abdobooks.com

abdobooks.com

Published by Abdo Publishing, a division of ABDO, PO Box 398166, Minneapolis, Minnesota 55439. Copyright © 2023 by Abdo Consulting Group, Inc. International copyrights reserved in all countries. No part of this book may be reproduced in any form without written permission from the publisher. SportsZone™ is a trademark and logo of Abdo Publishing.

Printed in the United States of America, North Mankato, Minnesota.
102022
012023

Cover Photo: Brian Rothmuller/Icon Sportswire/AP Images
Interior Photos: George Kubas/Diamond Images/Getty Images, 4; Universal History Archive/Universal Images Group/Getty Images, 6; George Rinhart/Corbis Historical/Getty Images, 8; Bruce Bennett/Getty Images Studios/Getty Images, 10; AP Images, 11, 14, 19; Major League Baseball/Getty Images, 13; Major League Baseball/Hulton Archive/Getty Images, 17, 26; Bettmann/Getty Images, 21, 24, 29; David Durochik/AP Images, 22; Tony Tomsic/AP Images, 28; Focus on Sport/Getty Images Sport/Getty Images, 31; John Reid III/MLB Photos/Getty Images Sport/Getty Images, 32; Jeff Haynes/AFP/Getty Images, 36; Aaron Harris/The Canadian Press/AP Images, 38; Matt Slocum/AP Images, 39; Joe Robbins/Icon Sportswire/AP Images, 41

Editor: Charlie Beattie
Series Designer: Becky Daum

Library of Congress Control Number: 2022940398

Publisher's Cataloging-in-Publication Data

Names: Hewson, Anthony K., author.
Title: Cleveland Guardians / by Anthony K. Hewson
Description: Minneapolis, Minnesota: Abdo Publishing, 2023 | Series: Inside MLB | Includes online resources and index.
Identifiers: ISBN 9781098290153 (lib. bdg.) | ISBN 9781098275358 (ebook)
Subjects: LCSH: Baseball teams--Juvenile literature. | Professional sports--Juvenile literature. | Sports franchises--Juvenile literature. | Major League Baseball (Organization)--Juvenile literature.
Classification: DDC 796.35764--dc23

TABLE OF

CONTENTS

CHAPTER 1

A NEW ERA

The red, white, and blue colors were the same. The front of the Cleveland jersey looked similar with its slanted lettering. But those letters spelled out something brand-new. After 107 years as the Indians, Cleveland's baseball team was changing its name.

Much had changed in that century. Ethnic nicknames such as Indians used to be common among sports teams. But many people had always seen these names as highly disrespectful. Over the years, calls to change such nicknames had grown louder and louder. And many teams in a similar spot had already chosen to abandon their tradition for something less offensive.

The "Guardians" logo appeared behind home plate and above the scoreboard at Progressive Field for the first time in 2022.

Under its previous name, Cleveland had been a large part of baseball history. The franchise had won two World Series and appeared in four others. But that didn't change the fact that the team could no longer justify a name that so many people found offensive. So, on November 19, 2021, the team announced its new era. From then on, Cleveland's historic baseball team would be known as the Guardians.

As the team said on social media, it was time for a new chapter of Cleveland baseball.

NAME GAME

Cleveland wasn't always known as the Indians. The team went by a variety of names in its early years. In its first season, in 1901, the team was officially called the Blues. But one of the local newspapers also referred to the group as the Babes, Spiders, and Buckeyes in various

Nap Lajoie won three batting titles in Cleveland, including the 1910 season when he hit .383.

articles. Another paper, in 1902, named them the Bronchos. In 1903 fans settled on "Naps" because of star player Napoleon "Nap" Lajoie.

Naming the team after Lajoie made sense. The second baseman was one of baseball's earliest superstars. He won four American League (AL) batting titles while with Cleveland. He also managed the team during some of his playing years.

When Lajoie left in 1915, the team needed a new name. It eventually selected Indians. The name was possibly a reference to Louis Sockalexis, a Penobscot athlete who had played for an earlier Cleveland team in the 1890s. Whatever the reason, the name stuck for the next 107 years.

ADDIE JOSS

Pitcher Addie Joss provided an early highlight in Cleveland history when he tossed a perfect game in 1908. Joss needed only 74 pitches to do it. He also threw a no-hitter in 1910. Joss's promising career came to a sudden end the next year. He died of tubercular meningitis at the age of 31.

TRAGEDY AND TRIUMPH

It was tough to replace a player like Lajoie. But center fielder Tris Speaker fit the bill. Speaker was in the prime of his career when he was traded to Cleveland by the Boston Red Sox before the 1916 season.

Ray Chapman's death led to several rule changes in baseball, including the banning of the spitball pitch.

Speaker won the 1916 AL batting title. He played 10 more years with Cleveland and hit .300 nine times. And like Lajoie before him, he also managed the team. Speaker took over in 1919.

The 1920 season got off to a great start. The club was in first place for most of the summer. But tragedy struck in August. Star shortstop Ray Chapman was hit in the head by a pitch from New York Yankees pitcher Carl Mays. Players in those days did not wear protective batting helmets. Chapman was taken to the hospital but died the next day. He was the first Major League Baseball (MLB) player to die from a pitched ball.

Chapman's death changed baseball in several ways. For example, before the incident, baseballs were rarely taken out of play. Because they were used longer, they became dirty and hard to see. After Chapman's death, rules were changed so that balls that got too dirty were immediately removed.

Cleveland carried on and finished the season strong. Taking Chapman's place at shortstop was 21-year-old rookie Joe Sewell. He hit .329 the rest of the year. It was the start of a Hall-of-Fame career. The team won the AL title to make it to the first World Series in club history. Its opponent was a team called the Brooklyn Robins, known today as the Los Angeles Dodgers.

A SERIES OF FIRSTS

One of Cleveland's strengths all year was its pitching staff. Jim Bagby, Stan Coveleski, and Ray Caldwell combined to win 75 games. Cleveland relied on each of them to be at their best in the World Series.

Game 1 was Coveleski's. He tamed the Robins lineup, allowing only five hits and one run in a complete game. Catcher Steve O'Neill drove in all the runs Cleveland needed.

Jim Bagby won 31 games for Cleveland during the 1920 season.

Bagby and Caldwell also pitched well. But the Cleveland lineup scored just one run combined in the next two games. Suddenly Cleveland was in trouble, down 2–1 in the best-of-nine series.

Coveleski won his second start in Game 4 to even things up. That set up an incredible Game 5. The final score of 8–1 made it the biggest blowout of the series. But in the nine innings, Cleveland managed to achieve three World Series "firsts." Right fielder Elmer Smith came up in the bottom of the first with the bases loaded. He blasted a 1–2 pitch from Brooklyn ace Burleigh Grimes over the right-field wall. It was the first Grand Slam in World Series history.

It was also the only run support Bagby needed. But that didn't stop the pitcher from adding another number to the scoreboard in the fourth. With two on and one out, Bagby

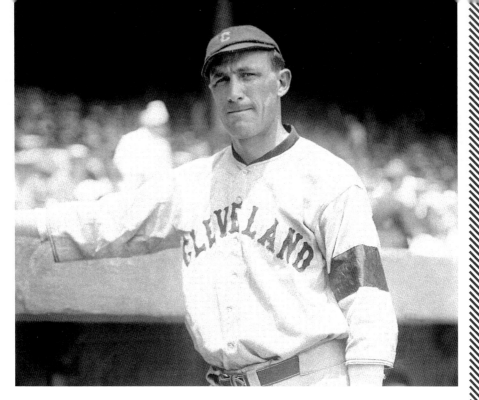

Bill Wambsganss hit only 4-for-26 in the 1920 World Series, but his triple play was a key to Cleveland's win.

took Grimes deep for the first-ever World Series home run by a pitcher.

Cleveland then added to the historic day on defense in the top of the fifth. Bagby allowed 13 hits on the day, including two Brooklyn singles to lead off the inning. The next batter, Clarence Mitchell, hit a hard line drive to Cleveland second baseman Bill Wambsganss. After touching second base to double off Pete Kilduff, Wambsganss tagged Otto Miller to end the inning. The unassisted triple play was the first triple play of any kind in the World Series. Even 100 years later, it remained the only triple play ever turned in the Fall Classic.

The Robins never recovered. Cleveland shut out Brooklyn in Games 6 and 7. Covaleski clinched the victory with his third win of the series. Cleveland celebrated its first championship in team history.

AWARDS AND HONORS

Cleveland finished second in the AL in 1921. But its 94 wins were not enough to overtake the New York Yankees. Until 1969 only the top team in each league went to the postseason. The rest of the decade belonged to New York. As Cleveland's stars aged, the team finished as high as second only once.

Instead, the city's fans celebrated individual feats. Speaker became the fifth member of the 3,000-hit club in May 1925. A year later, first baseman George Burns was AL Most Valuable Player (MVP). That year he racked up 64 doubles, breaking the old record of 59 held by Speaker.

By 1932 Cleveland was outgrowing its home of League Park. The team started playing games at Municipal Stadium, a huge building on the shores of Lake Erie. There, the team attracted MLB-record crowds of more than 80,000. For the next 15 years, the team split its time between the two stadiums. And in that time, some of the best players in team history emerged.

Tris Speaker retired as the all-time MLB leader in doubles, with 792.

CHAPTER 2

LAKE ERIE LEGENDS

By 1936 Cleveland's World Series glory days were long past. And while Cleveland had only one losing season in the 1930s, it never finished closer than 12 games out of first place.

However, in 1936 an exciting debut gave fans a look at the future. Pitcher Bob Feller was just 17 years old when he first took the mound on July 19. The teenager became an instant celebrity. Though he made only 14 appearances that year, *Time* magazine put him on its cover before the 1937 season. His blazing fastball quickly earned him the nickname "Rapid Robert." It also made him an All-Star in 1938. A year later, he

Bob Feller struck out 15 batters in his first MLB start in 1936. A month later, he set an AL record with 17 strikeouts in a game.

began a stretch of three straight seasons leading the AL in both wins and strikeouts.

To back up Feller's brilliance, Cleveland also had a mighty bat in shortstop Lou Boudreau. He played his first full season in 1940 and drove in 101 runs. Boudreau also had a great glove and even served as manager from 1942 to 1950.

The 1940 team had a chance to win the AL going into the final series of the season with the first-place Detroit Tigers. Feller started the first game of the series and allowed only two runs. But Cleveland couldn't score any and was eliminated from the race.

It was Cleveland's best season since 1921. But just when things were looking up, the team fell back into fourth place in 1941. Then it got an even bigger shock. The now 23-year-old Feller sacrificed prime years of his career to serve his country in World War II (1939–45).

MOVE TO MUNICIPAL

Feller missed three full seasons serving in the military. He came back for part of the 1945 season after the conflict ended. When 1946 opened, Feller went back to dominating on the mound. He led the AL in wins and strikeouts yet again.

By then Cleveland had a new owner. Bill Veeck had grown up in baseball. His father was the president of the Chicago

Cubs. Veeck was new to MLB ownership but had owned the minor league Milwaukee Brewers. It was there that he got the reputation as a master promoter.

Veeck allowed fans to get married at home plate. He gave away live animals as prizes. He had the idea to play morning games to attract fans who worked nights.

One of Veeck's biggest ideas for Cleveland was

Larry Doby was the first Black player ever to hit a home run in an MLB World Series game.

moving into the much larger Municipal Stadium full time. The stadium also had lights, allowing the team to play night games. With the night contests came regular fireworks shows, another of Veeck's new ideas.

Veeck was also progressive in signing players. In 1947 Jackie Robinson became the first Black MLB player since the modern era of MLB began in 1901. Right behind Robinson was Cleveland's Larry Doby. Veeck signed the second baseman

VEECK AND DOBY

Many white MLB players were upset by the idea of Black players joining teams in the late 1940s. Bill Veeck made sure that wasn't an issue for Larry Doby in Cleveland. As Doby put it, "One by one, (Indians manager) Lou (Boudreau) introduced me to each player. All the guys put their hand out—all but three. As soon as he could, Bill Veeck got rid of those three."

after Doby had starred for the Newark Eagles of the Negro Leagues, where Black players had to play before MLB opened up to them. Doby made his MLB debut in July, just three months after Robinson, as the first Black player in the AL. He struggled in 29 games his first year. But after moving to center field in 1948, Doby broke out as a star.

RETURN TO RELEVANCE

Led by an MVP season from Boudreau, Cleveland was in the running for the AL title in 1948. Feller was having a solid season along with fellow starters Bob Lemon and Gene Bearden, but the team needed more pitching. Veeck signed Satchel Paige, who was perhaps the greatest star the Negro Leagues ever produced. Now the righty would get his chance in MLB.

Some people accused Veeck of signing Paige only as a promotional stunt. No one knew exactly how old Paige was, but most thought he was around 41 or 42. But Paige soon showed he had plenty left in his arm. Baseball's oldest rookie went 6–1 down the stretch and helped Cleveland keep up with the Boston Red Sox in the pennant race.

On the season's last day, Feller started against the Detroit Tigers with a chance to clinch the AL title. But he struggled in a 7–1 loss. Boston won to force a one-game playoff the next day.

In Boston's Fenway Park, Boudreau got Cleveland off to a great start with a first-inning home run. He added a second in the fifth inning, and Cleveland won 8–3 to head back to the World Series.

Satchel Paige posted a 10–8 record and a 2.78 ERA in parts of two seasons with Cleveland.

Cleveland didn't have to travel at all for Game 1. Its opponent was Boston's NL team, the Braves. Feller finally got his chance to pitch in the World Series after nine MLB seasons. He dominated in Game 1, allowing just one run. But Cleveland didn't score any against Braves ace Johnny Sain in a 1–0 loss.

Cleveland pitchers allowed only three runs in the next three games. And the offense did just enough to win all three.

Feller took the mound in Game 5 with a chance to close it out in front of the home crowd. But this time the ace was pounded in an 11–5 loss.

Cleveland had another chance to close out the series back in Boston for Game 6 when it built a 4–1 lead in the eighth. Boston quickly got two runs back to make it 4–3. But Bearden, who went 20–7 during the season, closed out the inning with the lead still intact. After Cleveland went in order in the ninth, Bearden returned to the mound. He gave up a leadoff walk. But the next hitter popped up a bunt attempt. Catcher Jim Hegan caught it and doubled the runner off first. Bearden got the final out, and Cleveland was a winner again.

CAUGHT OUT

Cleveland got off to a slow start in 1949 and never got into first place. The team finished in third, eight games back. Veeck wished to literally bury the past. He had the team's 1948 championship flag buried so the team would focus on the future. But there was no future in Cleveland for Veeck. Struggling for money, he sold the team soon after.

Despite winning more than 90 games each year from 1950 to 1953, Cleveland could not get past the dominant Yankees in the AL. That all changed in 1954. Cleveland looked good heading into the year. Doby was now a star, and third

Owner Bill Veeck, *left*, and several Cleveland players mob Gene Bearden, *center*, after the pitcher saved the clinching Game 6 of the 1948 World Series.

baseman Al Rosen was coming off an MVP season in 1953. When the regular season was over, the team looked even better. The Yankees finished 103–51. But that was only good enough to finish eight games back of 111–43 Cleveland.

Al Rosen had league highs of 43 home runs and 115 RBIs during his MVP season in 1953.

The 97–57 New York Giants were waiting in the World Series.

Many people thought Cleveland would win easily. And in Game 1, the team went up 2–0. But the Giants tied the game in the third. Cleveland had a chance to take the lead in the eighth. With runners on first and second and no one out, first baseman Vic Wertz smashed a fly ball to deep center field. Giants center fielder Willie Mays sprinted to track it down in the huge center field at the Polo Grounds, New York's home stadium. With his back to the infield, he made an over-the-shoulder catch to keep the score tied. Mays's incredible grab is known today simply as "the Catch." The rest of the series also went New York's way. The Giants surprisingly swept Cleveland. It would be a while before Cleveland got a shot at another title.

RECORD CROWDS

Cleveland's move to Municipal Stadium came at a time when the team was winning a lot. And Municipal had room for all the fans who wanted to come see those wins. The biggest crowd in MLB history came out for a doubleheader on September 12, 1954. More than 86,000 fans packed into the lakefront stadium.

A CURSE?

The 1950s were a time of change in Cleveland. Lou Boudreau, Larry Doby, and Bob Feller all left the team or retired. The changes would only increase with the arrival of "Trader Frank."

Cleveland hired Frank Lane as general manager after the 1957 season. Lane was known for one thing: making deals. Sometimes they worked out. With the Chicago White Sox, he traded catcher Aaron Robinson for pitcher Billy Pierce in 1948. Robinson was out of the majors by 1952. Pierce made seven All-Star teams.

Lane made some good deals in Cleveland too. He traded Doby, in his second stint with the team, for outfielder Tito

Lou Boudreau was the 1948 AL MVP while also serving as Cleveland's manager. His retirement in 1950 was part of a major transition for the team.

Francona in 1959. Doby's career lasted just 39 more games, while Francona became an All-Star.

However, there were plenty of deals that did not work out for Cleveland. Lane traded first baseman Norm Cash only to see him slug nearly 400 home runs for the Detroit Tigers. Lane sent outfielder Roger Maris to the Kansas City Athletics in 1958, only to see Maris break the single-season home run record in 1961 as a New York Yankee. But one trade was the final straw for Cleveland fans.

Rocky Colavito hit 129 home runs in just four seasons during his first stint in Cleveland.

A ROCKY TRADE

Outfielder Rocky Colavito led the AL in homers in 1959. He made his first All-Star team and was an MVP contender. But just before the 1960 season, Lane shipped him off to Detroit for outfielder Harvey Kuenn.

Kuenn was a good player. He had just won the AL batting title with a .353 average. But Colavito was a beloved fan favorite. Fans called the team nonstop to complain about the trade.

Their anger showed in the 1960 attendance. The team sold 500,000 fewer tickets. That anger increased when Kuenn played one injury-plagued season in Cleveland. Lane traded Kuenn in December 1960. One month later, Lane quit. In the years that followed, many fans came to believe that the trade cursed Cleveland.

Cleveland attempted to right its wrong in 1965. New general manager Gabe Paul got Colavito back. But he had to give up outfielder Tommie Agee and pitcher Tommy John to do it. Agee became the 1966 AL Rookie of the Year and later helped the New York Mets win the 1969 World Series. And John won nearly 300 more career games.

Colavito did make two more All-Star teams, but he did so on bad teams. By the time he left for good in 1967, Cleveland was among the worst teams in baseball. It would stay that way for the next 25 years.

HISTORY MADE

While the team struggled, there were still plenty of highlights for fans. In October 1974, the team that signed Doby and

Frank Robinson instructs his players from the Cleveland dugout.

Satchel Paige made another history-making moment. Cleveland hired Frank Robinson to be the first Black manager in MLB history.

Robinson was a Hall of Famer as a player, a 14-time All-Star who was traded to Cleveland in September 1974. Just a few weeks later, the team made him manager while he was still playing.

Robinson's debut as a manager came on April 8, 1975. General manager Phil Seghi took Robinson aside and told him to hit a homer in his first at-bat. Robinson couldn't believe it. But hours later, he blasted a 2–2 fastball deep to left field. The home crowd went wild as Robinson rounded the bases. There were few other highlights that year as Cleveland went 79–80. But memories like that kept fans coming back.

A HOME OF THEIR OWN

On May 15, 1981, Cleveland pitcher Len Barker tossed a perfect game at Municipal Stadium. It was just the 10th perfect game in MLB history. And it was the first by a Cleveland pitcher since Addie Joss in 1908. Unfortunately, only 7,290 supporters were there to see it.

Len Barker's 1981 perfect game was the highlight of his only All-Star season in the major leagues.

Years of losing had taken its toll on Cleveland fans. Municipal Stadium was still the largest ballpark in baseball, but the team struggled to attract 1,000,000 spectators per year. It was also aging, needed repairs, and lacked many features of modern stadiums. The biggest issue was that the team also had to share it with football's Cleveland Browns. The stadium wasn't truly designed for baseball.

Cleveland's baseball team had thought about leaving the city before. And when the team went up for sale in the 1980s, fans again worried the club might finally bolt. But brothers Richard and David Jacobs purchased the franchise in 1986 to keep it in Cleveland. A new stadium deal came together in 1990. The new park, built in downtown, would be just for baseball.

COVER CURSE

Cleveland had a surprising winning record in 1986. Some people, including the writers of *Sports Illustrated* magazine, thought they would do well in 1987 too. *Sports Illustrated* featured Cleveland on a cover before the season. The magazine called them the AL's best team. But Cleveland couldn't live up to that prediction. The team lost 101 games and finished in last place.

THE JAKE

On the field, Cleveland was also starting to make progress. John Hart was hired as manager for 19 games late in 1989. In 1990 he moved into the team's front office to help rebuild its talent.

The way to do that was through trades. Catcher Sandy Alomar and infielder Carlos Baerga came in deals after the 1989 season. Alomar was Rookie of the Year in 1990. Both players turned into All-Stars. Hart dealt for athletic center fielder Kenny Lofton a year later. He was runner-up for Rookie of the Year in 1992 and a future All-Star and Gold Glove winner for defense.

The team also developed its own stars. Outfielder Manny Ramírez was the team's first draft pick in 1991. By 1994 he was runner-up for Rookie of the Year. That same year, Cleveland began its new era.

Jacobs Field opened on April 4, 1994. President Bill Clinton was there to throw out the first pitch. The home team gave fans at "the Jake" a thrill with a 4–3 win in extra innings. It was the start of something big.

Cleveland had added first baseman Eddie Murray and pitcher Dennis

Kenny Lofton was one of several young stars that arrived in Cleveland during the early 1990s.

Martínez as veteran signings. It had also traded for defensive wizard Omar Vizquel at shortstop. The team raced out to a 66–47 record. However, the end of the 1994 season was canceled due to a player's strike. There was no World Series.

Baseball eventually came back, though. And when the players and owners reached a deal to play in 1995, Cleveland looked like a true contender.

CHAPTER 4

CHANGING TIMES

Fans were disappointed to miss seeing what their team could do for the rest of 1994. But the team picked up right where it left off in 1995. Cleveland started off 1–2. But that was the last time the team had a losing record that season.

Cleveland never lost more than nine games in a month. The team was 41–17 at the end of June and went on to win its division by 30 games. Manny Ramírez hit 31 homers while fellow outfielder Albert Belle mashed 50.

A full house packed Jacobs Field for Cleveland's first postseason game in 41 years. The Boston Red Sox jumped out to a 2–0 lead. Cleveland responded with three runs in the bottom of the fifth. Eventually Boston tied it up, and the

Manny Ramírez finished second in the 1994 Rookie of the Year race after driving in 60 runs in just 91 games.

game went to extra innings. Boston took the lead again in the 11th. Belle saved the day by crushing a game-tying homer to left. Two innings later, backup catcher Tony Peña won it with another homer. Days later, Cleveland finished off a three-game sweep.

The Seattle Mariners awaited in the AL Championship Series (ALCS). Despite losing two of the first three games, Cleveland rallied to win the series. Seattle was held to two total runs in Cleveland's final three wins.

The toughest test came in the World Series. The Atlanta Braves had one of the best pitching staffs in baseball. Cleveland lost close games to fall behind 2–0.

Back at Jacobs Field, it was a different story. Cleveland hitters jumped on Atlanta starter John Smoltz. But a back-and-forth game eventually went to extra innings. In the 11th, Eddie Murray singled to score the winning run and keep Cleveland's hopes alive.

THE 455 PLAQUE

Like all teams, Cleveland has honored some of its greatest players by retiring their uniform numbers so no one will ever wear them again. Bob Feller's 19 and Lou Boudreau's 5 are among nine that hang in the outfield at Progressive Field. But the No. 455 looks a little odd. That wasn't a player's number but the number of games in a row Cleveland fans sold out Jacobs Field, as the stadium was known at the time. The streak, once an MLB record, began on June 12, 1995, and continued until April 4, 2001.

After losing Game 4, Cleveland had another offensive outburst to win Game 5. But Cleveland managed just a single hit in eight innings against Atlanta lefty Tom Glavine in Game 6. The 1–0 loss ended Cleveland's magical season.

TWO OUTS AWAY

Cleveland won its division for the third year in a row in 1997. But the team won just 86 games. That was the worst record of any AL playoff team. Underdogs in the playoffs, Cleveland took its fans on an unexpected run. It started with an upset of the defending world-champion New York Yankees in the division series.

In the ALCS, Cleveland faced the Baltimore Orioles, who had knocked them out of the playoffs the year before. After five close games, Cleveland held a 3–2 lead before Game 6 in Baltimore.

Another tense game went into extra innings tied 0–0. Cleveland had only two hits. But in the 11th, with two outs, second baseman Tony Fernández turned on the first pitch he saw. It soared out of the park to right field to give Cleveland a 1–0 lead. Star closer José Mesa then got the final three outs.

One of baseball's oldest teams faced off with its newest in the World Series. Cleveland took on the Florida Marlins, who had been founded in 1993. The series shifted back and forth

Cleveland shortstop Omar Vizquel avoids Florida's Gary Sheffield while turning a double play during the 1997 World Series.

from warm, muggy Miami to frigid Cleveland. In Game 4, the temperature dipped below freezing at Jacobs Field.

The teams also went back and forth, trading wins until a deciding Game 7 was set for Miami. Despite taking an early 2–0 lead, Cleveland could not add on. The Marlins scored runs in the seventh and ninth innings to tie it up. Eventually, in the 11th, Florida won the game on a walk-off single. As the young Marlins celebrated, Cleveland fans dealt with the frustration of being two outs from ending a now 49-year title drought.

A NEW ERA

A big reason Cleveland remained an AL contender was Ramírez, who was one of the best power hitters in baseball. Ramírez hit 127 homers from 1998 to 2000. But the 2000 season also saw Cleveland miss the playoffs for the first time since 1993. Ramírez was a free agent and chose to sign with the Boston Red Sox. Cleveland also lost Sandy Alomar to the rival Chicago White Sox.

The 2001 season was the last for John Hart. Cleveland topped the division again but was eliminated in the first round of the playoffs. New general manager Mark Shapiro looked to start over.

Shapiro traded some of the team's veterans for young players. Ace pitcher Bartolo Colón brought back promising young outfielder Grady Sizemore and pitcher Cliff Lee. Veteran pitcher Chuck Finley was dealt for speedy outfielder Coco Crisp. Cleveland fell to 68 wins in 2003 but was back on top of the division by 2007. However, the city suffered more playoff heartbreak when Cleveland let a 3–1 ALCS lead slip away to Boston.

WORLD CLASS AGAIN

Cleveland continued to cycle out older players for younger prospects. Lee was traded for pitcher Carlos Carrasco in

Cliff Lee finished 22–3 with a 2.54 ERA while winning the 2008 Cy Young Award in Cleveland.

2009, and Carrasco turned into the team's new ace. Shapiro also acquired star pitchers Trevor Bauer and Corey Kluber as Cleveland worked its way back up the standings.

Cleveland also drafted well. All-Star shortstop Francisco Lindor was the team's top pick in 2011. Cleveland discovered slugging third baseman José Ramírez as a teenage phenomenon in the Dominican Republic. Pitching and clutch hitting were how Cleveland got back to the top of the division in 2016. But Shapiro wasn't there to see it. He had taken the job of leading the Toronto Blue Jays a year earlier.

Rajai Davis, *left*, is congratulated by his teammates after his game-tying home run in Game 7 of the 2016 World Series.

Cleveland kicked off the playoffs with a thrilling sweep of the Red Sox. Then it was a meeting with Shapiro's Blue Jays. Cleveland easily brushed aside Toronto in five games. Cleveland had another shot at ending its long championship dry spell.

The team's World Series opponents were the Chicago Cubs, another team looking to reverse its ugly championship history. Chicago hadn't won it all since 1908. Both teams battled hard, and the series was very close. Cleveland went up 3–1 but lost two in a row as the series went to a Game 7.

Cleveland fell behind 5–1 at home but battled back to tie it on a home run by outfielder Rajai Davis in the eighth inning. The game went to extra innings. To add to the drama, a brief rainstorm delayed play before the tenth. Cleveland pitcher Bryan Shaw, one of the team's top relievers, allowed two runs to give Chicago an 8–6 lead.

Cleveland wasn't done. The winning run came to the plate in the bottom of the 10th. But the Cubs shut the door, and Cleveland had to settle for second place again.

STANDING GUARD

Cleveland remained a contender in the division but couldn't repeat its success in the playoffs. That was despite José Ramírez becoming a yearly MVP threat. The third baseman remained the team's key player even as the roster changed around him.

An even bigger change took place off the field. For years, the team had been pressured to change its Indians nickname and logo. While use of terms for Indigenous peoples as sports nicknames was common when Cleveland was founded, such names were widely seen as racist in modern times.

Cleveland chose to honor a local landmark with its new nickname. "Guardians" references statues on a bridge close to

Jose Ramírez made his fourth All-Star team in 2022.

the ballpark that Clevelanders know and love. It was a name that all fans could enjoy. They hoped that the new name would bring a long-awaited championship with it.

TIMELINE

1901

Using a variety of names, Cleveland's baseball team plays its first season as an original member of the American League.

1915

Cleveland adopts the nickname Indians, which it will stick with for more than 100 years.

1920

Cleveland wins its first AL title and beats the Brooklyn Robins to win its first World Series.

1926

First baseman George Burns wins the first AL MVP award in Cleveland history.

1936

Seventeen-year-old pitcher Bob Feller makes his first of 484 starts for Cleveland.

1947

Under new owner Bill Veeck, Cleveland makes history by signing Negro League star Larry Doby, who becomes the first Black player in the AL later that season.

1948

With the help of Negro League star Satchel Paige, Cleveland wins the AL again and knocks off the Boston Braves in the World Series.

1954

Cleveland makes it back to the World Series, but is swept by Willie Mays and the New York Giants.

1960

General manager Frank Lane makes a disastrous trade of outfielder Rocky Colavito, leading some fans to believe the team is cursed as Cleveland enters a period of decline.

1974

Cleveland hires legendary slugger Frank Robinson as player/manager. Robinson becomes the first Black manager in MLB history when he leads the team out on Opening Day 1975.

1981

Len Barker pitches the second perfect game in team history.

1994

Cleveland opens its new downtown ballpark, Jacobs Field.

1995

Cleveland makes the World Series but loses in six games to the Atlanta Braves.

1997

Cleveland gets two outs away from winning the World Series but blows the lead in Game 7 to lose to the Florida Marlins.

2016

Facing the Chicago Cubs, Cleveland has a 3–1 lead in the World Series but loses in seven games.

2021

Cleveland announces it is changing its name to Guardians and discontinuing use of all Indigenous imagery.

TEAM FACTS

FRANCHISE HISTORY

Cleveland Blues (1901)
Cleveland Bronchos (1902)
Cleveland Naps (1903–14)
Cleveland Indians (1915–2021)
Cleveland Guardians (2022–)

WORLD SERIES CHAMPIONSHIPS

1920, 1948

KEY PLAYERS

Sandy Alomar (1990–2000)
Earl Averill (1929–39)
Lou Boudreau (1938–50)
Rocky Colavito (1955–59, 1965–67)
Stan Coveleski (1916–24)
Larry Doby (1947–55, 1958)
Bob Feller (1936–41, 1945–56)
Nap Lajoie (1902–14)
Francisco Lindor (2015–20)
Kenny Lofton (1992–96, 1998–2001, 2007)
José Ramírez (2013–)
Manny Ramírez (1993–2000)

Joe Sewell (1920–30)
Tris Speaker (1916–26)
Jim Thome (1991–2002, 2011)
Early Wynn (1949–57, 1963)

KEY MANAGERS

Lou Boudreau (1942–50)
Terry Francona (2013–)
Al Lopez (1951–56)
Tris Speaker (1919–26)

HOME STADIUMS

League Park (1901–32, 1934–46)
  Also known as:
  Dunn Field (1916–27)
Municipal Stadium (1932–33, 1937–93)
Progressive Field (1994–)
  Also known as:
  Jacobs Field (1994–2008)

TEAM TRIVIA

BAD REPUTATION

Before the Guardians existed, Cleveland had an American Association/National League team from 1887 to 1899 called the Spiders. The team's last season was one of the worst major league baseball has ever seen. The Spiders finished with a record of 20–134 in 1899.

ON THE SILVER SCREEN

Cleveland was featured in the 1989 film *Major League*. But the movie was filmed in Milwaukee, with the Brewers' County Stadium playing the role of Municipal Stadium.

INTERLEAGUE RIVALS

Since 1997 Cleveland has played in-state rival Cincinnati for the Ohio Cup. Whichever team wins more games in their yearly series wins the trophy.

FEEL THE BEAT

Starting in the 1970s, a familiar drumming sound could be heard in the background of Cleveland home games. That was fan John Adams, who has played his bass drum at most home games ever since.

GLOSSARY

ace

A team's best starting pitcher.

closer

A pitcher who comes in at the end of the game to secure a win for his team.

clutch

An important or pressure-packed situation.

complete game

A game in which a starting pitcher stays in the entire game without being relieved.

general manager

An executive who runs a team and is responsible for finding and signing players.

indigenous

Relating to the earliest known residents of an area

minor league

A lower level of baseball where players work on improving their skills before they reach the major leagues.

perfect game

A complete game in which a team retires every opposing batter and allows no base runners.

progressive

Forward thinking and interested in new ideas.

upset

An unexpected victory by a supposedly weaker team or player.

veteran

A player who has played for many years.

walk-off

Any victory in which the home team scores the winning run in the bottom of the final inning.

MORE INFORMATION

BOOKS

Flynn, Brendan. *The MLB Encyclopedia*. Minneapolis, MN: Abdo Publishing, 2022.

Gitlin, Marty. *MLB*. Minneapolis, MN: Abdo Publishing, 2021.

Harris, Duchess, JD, PhD, with Alex Kies. *The Negro Leagues*. Abdo Publishing, 2020.

ONLINE RESOURCES

To learn more about the Cleveland Guardians, please visit **abdobooklinks.com** or scan this QR code. These links are routinely monitored and updated to provide the most current information available.

INDEX

ABOUT THE AUTHOR

Anthony K. Hewson is a freelance writer who specializes in writing nonfiction for kids.